Breaking the Language Barrier

Breaking the Language Barrier

*The essential guide to learning
Western European languages*

by

Georgina Howard

Breaking the Language Barrier

First published 2001 by

SIMON & SIMON Publishing Limited

117 Walton Street, London SW3 2HP

Tel: 020 7584 8833 Fax: 020 7591 0060

Email: info@simonandsimon.co.uk

All rights reserved. No part of this publication may be reproduced, stored in a retrieval system, or transmitted, in any form or by any means, electronic, mechanical, photocopying, recording, or otherwise, without the prior permission of the copyright owner.

Copyright © SIMON & SIMON Publishing Limited 2001

ISBN 0-9541203-0-2

British Library Cataloguing in Publication Data
A catalogue record for this book is available from the British Library

Illustrations by John Longstaff

Printed by Imperial Printers UK Limited, Twickenham

Design & typesetting by Teamwork, Sompting, West Sussex

Contents

	List of Abbreviations	7
	Introduction – *Linguaphobia!*	9
	Why are the British, intrepid travellers and adventurers, often defeated by learning a foreign language?	
1	**Sizing up the Language Barrier**	13
	The three principles of learning. What do we – and don't we – need to learn? And how exactly do we do it?	
2	**A Brief History of the English Language**	21
	In exploring the history of the English language we unearth the thousands of words and structures it has in common with the languages of our European neighbours.	
3	**A Brief Tour of English Grammar**	33
	Many British people are intimidated by the word 'grammar' but with a clearer overview of how it works, learning the next language is not nearly as complex.	
4	**Breaking the Barrier: The Romance Languages (*French, Italian and Spanish*)**	43
	How did the Romance languages originate, and what characteristics do they share with English? What are the five fundamental differences in grammar between English and the Romance languages?	

5	**Breaking the Barrier: The Germanic Languages** *(German, Dutch and Danish)*	53

How did the Germanic languages originate, and what characteristics do they share with English? What are the five fundamental differences in grammar between English and the Germanic languages?

6	**Action Plan**	63

Which is the right course for you? What are its advantages and pitfalls? Here is a range of language and study tips as well as practical advice on how to get started.

7	**Being Culturally Aware**	71

What are the principal areas where cultural misunderstandings arise?

	Bon Voyage	75
	Glossary	76

Abbreviations

The following abbreviations have been used in the book:

Da	Modern Danish
Du	Modern Dutch
F	Modern French
G	Modern German
It	Modern Italian
Sp	Modern Spanish
Frn	Words of French origin
Gmc	Words of Germanic origin

Introduction – *Linguaphobia!*

This book is intended as a short, colourful and eye-opening introduction to Western European languages, aimed at the thousands of people who have longed to learn them but have lacked the confidence to do so. It sets out to dispel the myths surrounding foreign-language learning and reveal the many similarities that exist between English and the languages of our European neighbours.

It is dedicated to people who enjoy travelling but are constantly frustrated by their inability to communicate with the local people. It is for the holidaymaker who likes to wander off the beaten track, explore medieval villages, sip *cappuccino al fresco* and amble from *fiesta* to *siesta*, *château* to *café*. It will also benefit the international business person – who, invited to dinner at the end of a meeting, realises the need for a new range of language tools.

Despite the steady process of internationalisation, many people still seem afraid of learning a foreign language. Why is this? What are the roots of the problem? Why do the British suffer so acutely from *linguaphobia*?

On my travels I meet a stream of intrepid Brits. They trek the Himalayas in thunderstorms, raft the Zambezi with crocodiles and yet, no matter how extrovert and gregarious they are by nature, one obstacle seems always to obstruct their path – *the language barrier*. Excuses such as 'my memory is terrible' or 'I just don't have the ear', crop up time and time again. To some extent we can blame our colonial past; rather than adapting to foreign cultures we have forced them to adapt to ours and suffered the consequence – a national apathy towards the learning of foreign languages.

Yet it is not only the apathetic who suffer from phobias. It is those who struggle valiantly to remedy the problem, braving a few phrases of a new language and bracing themselves for the reply, which finally comes – broken and faltering perhaps – but almost inevitably in English. One morning, at a baker's in Copenhagen, I remember asking, in Danish, for a couple of *Wienerbrød*.[1] The woman replied in English, I battled on in Danish; she asserted herself in English, I gritted my teeth and continued in Danish; she gritted hers and persisted in English and so we went on until I finally left the shop.

One of the great barriers we have to overcome is that most other Europeans are, of necessity, streets ahead of us in learning foreign languages, and in particular English. Many look for any opportunity to try out their English skills and we – demoralised and deflated – understandably give in.

However, this is not the whole picture. Another reason for our linguaphobia is the simple fact that we know so little about our own language. Most of us have little idea of how English is made up: we know nothing of *pronouns* and *prepositions*, and the word *grammar* fills us with horror as we recall images of clinical classrooms and military verb drills. Usually, it is only when we come to learn a foreign language that we gain our first real insight into our mother tongue. This seems to me a little like putting the cart before the horse or – as they say in Spanish – before the ox (*poner el carro delante de los bueyes*)!

Unfortunately, from the point of view of the non-native English-speaker our general ignorance of foreign languages is frequently interpreted as arrogance. In learning a few phrases of the local language we offer other cultures an important token of respect and show people that we are prepared to meet them on their terms, rather than expecting them to surrender to our own. From our perspective, no matter how well other people speak English, the ability to speak their native tongue allows us a far

---

[1] What we term Danish pastries, the Danes call *Wienerbrød*, which translates literally as 'Viennese bread'!

deeper insight into the nuances of their culture and values. It enables those wonderful impromptu conversations with locals in shops, on trains and walks around town, and inevitably enhances our ability to build solid friendships and business relationships.

This book does not set out to teach any language in particular (there are thousands of books and courses that do that). It does aim, however, to put the horse back in front of the cart by showing people what they do know before teaching them what they don't. It will help demystify Western European languages by revealing their many similarities with English, and provide people with the tools to help them make the most of the linguistic journey ahead of them. Are you ready? If you would rather launch yourself into conversation at the risk of error than remain tongue-tied in the search for perfection, then I warmly invite you to read on.

I'M NOT SO SURE ABOUT THIS, CREVASSE SOUNDS A BIT TOO FRENCH TO ME

Chapter One

Sizing up the Language Barrier

The Three Principles of Learning:

Use what you know as a foundation for what you don't know.

Seek the bigger picture before going into detail.

Start with the most important structures and leave the least important until last.

1. Use what you know as a foundation for what you don't know.

It is always easier to learn something new if we can liken it to something we already know. When it comes to languages, English-speakers often overlook the fact that they are already fluent speakers of the English language – one of the richest languages in the world. However, these language skills are acquired naturally rather than learned, and usually we reach adulthood with little formal understanding of the structures of our mother tongue. In taking time to examine English in more depth we find ourselves with an invaluable springboard into understanding the words and structures of the next language – especially when the language to be studied is so closely related to our own.

Look at the similarities between the following words:

Present:	*present (French), presente (Italian), presente (Spanish)*
House:	*Haus (German), hus (Danish), huis (Dutch)*

Illustration: *illustration (F), illustrazione (It), illustración (Sp), Illustration (G), illustration (Da), illustratie (Du)*

Warped by time, the similarities are not always immediately evident, but having learned where to look for them, and how to decipher the codes, they appear again and again.

School: *école (F), scuola (It), escuela (Sp)*
Book: *Buch (G), boek (Du), bog (Da)*

Seeking out similarities between words can be a great memory aid – or *aide-mémoire* (F). To remember a new word the brain likes to associate it with something it already knows, perhaps an existing word or concept with which it shares certain similarities. Creating links in this way acts like a kind of filing system and helps us to retrieve the word when we need it. For example the words 'constipated' in English, and *constipado* in Spanish (which means 'to have a cold'), initially have little in common. Yet, a little free association starts to reveal similarities, such as the common concept of 'being bunged up'. Can you find – or create – any conceptual links between the English word 'embarrassed' and the Spanish word *embarazada*, (which means 'to be pregnant')?

When there are no clear links between a new item of vocabulary and an English word, we can concoct eccentric stories or conjure up humorous pictures that help us recall the words. A typical situation is the difficulty we encounter when trying to remember a foreign name. I met a woman the other day called Rayhop and had to visualise a woman wearing dark *Ray*ban sunglasses that *hop*ped up and down on her nose. I didn't forget her name, although the mental picture was rather incongruous in a business meeting!

The following chapter on the history of the English language reveals the common roots shared by English and other Western European languages. In understanding their similarities, many foreign words then become instantly recognisable.

2. Seek the bigger picture before going into detail.

I have a road atlas that has been grossly mistreated over the years and is now missing the first two pages. These are unfortunately the two pages that give the overview of the whole of the British Isles. Trying to plan a journey from London to Edinburgh is now a rather laborious affair, flicking from one page to the next, following road after road, until I finally discover the route that takes me there most directly. Had these pages been there I would have known this at a glance; I would have had an immediate overview of the journey ahead, the distance, the choice of routes to get there and the stopping places along the way. For all tasks – from planning a journey to learning a language – having a feel for the bigger picture is essential. It tells us what to expect so that there are fewer surprises to throw us off-balance, and enables us to make informed choices and set ourselves realistic objectives. Unfortunately, traditional language teaching methods rarely give an overview of a language and you can find yourself plunged into the details within minutes, with no idea of how they fit into the greater scheme of things and how important they are to your individual goals. Led blindly from structure to structure you soon start to drag your feet, losing confidence along the way and falling deeper into the clutches of linguaphobia.

To help remedy this the chapters on the Romance and Germanic languages give a short overview of each language group, comparing and contrasting their main characteristics with those of the English language.

3. Start with the most important structures and leave the least important till last.

Once you have a general overview of the language you are studying, you need to decide exactly what your language aspirations are. Do you want to be able to converse with local people on a day to day basis? Or are you aiming to read history books in the original version? Deciding what you need to know and – just as importantly – what you don't need to know, is a very important step. Whatever your objectives, you will need to start by getting to grips with the most essential structures of the language and learning how to put a sentence together. Then, as your skills increase, you can gradually turn your focus towards the details. A passion for perfection can often get in the way at this point, and is far better replaced with a simple desire to communicate, using props, body language and a good dose of creative thinking.

Certain concepts are easier to convey than others. Racking your brains to remember whether to say *le vin* or *la vin* (*le* and *la* being equivalents in French for the word 'the') is probably an inefficient use of your energies at the start, and too much procrastination may mean missing out altogether! If you do say *la vin,* instead of *le vin,* it is hardly likely that the waiter will turn up with a mug of hot chocolate! On the other hand, learning the difference in French between 'I want', *je veux,* and 'I don't want', *je ne veux pas,* may be far more useful! Of course you should aspire to being grammatically correct, but initially it is more important to get beyond the fear of making a mistake and to focus your efforts on the most essential structures, leaving more complex language skills till later. In short, certain expressions can be **recognised** at the outset and then **learned** with time, others are better **recognised** and **learned** right from the start. These are highlighted throughout the book.

Adopting these three principles of learning will help you get the most from whatever course of study you choose, and ultimately enable you to teach yourself. In addition to these, we have another useful resource at our disposal, creative thinking.

Creative Thinking

Traditionally, school curricula have tended to channel pupils into Arts or Science streams, and years on many of us still categorise ourselves accordingly. Depending on whether we see ourselves as artistic or scientific we tend to embrace certain subjects and reject others. However, learning a language draws on both types of skills. It requires an element of logic and systematic thinking, as well as the ability to think creatively.

A sense of logic is necessary to apply one grammatical structure to a variety of situations and to deduce patterns and rules. Even if we see ourselves as scatterbrained, we all possess a sense of logic in order to survive. In fact, studies of children have proved that we are all born with an innate sense of grammar.[2] A child soon learns that by putting an '-ed' on the end of a verb he or she can talk in the past tense (talk – talked; ask – asked; play – played) and, on learning this new trick, applies it indiscriminately. This naturally causes problems on the few occasions that languages don't follow the rules, which is why young children can be heard to say 'he *taked* the dog' or 'Mummy *eated* the chocolate' (and why adults learning a new language often end up making similar mistakes).

Our ability to think creatively also plays an invaluable role, and even if we don't see ourselves as creative in the traditional sense, the ability to solve problems, remember odd pieces of information or plan dinner parties all require an element of creative thinking. Unfortunately, when embarking on something new we often lose our confidence at some stage and our creativity is quick to follow suit. Yet it is precisely these moments when our creative thinking can be put to best effect. In the case of foreign languages we tend to cling instinctively to the few expressions we have learnt by heart. Many of us are familiar with trying to compose a sentence, only to falter when we don't know – or are unable to recall – the very words we need to make ourselves understood.

What do we do?

Some may revert to English in embarrassment. Others will try again, searching for different ways to reformulate the sentence and get the meaning across. Negatives are often a good first step; if you have forgotten the word for 'closed' you can always relaunch the sentence with 'not open'. You have to think creatively.

A useful technique to develop is to try to view a situation from as many different perspectives as possible. If you are strug-

---

2   Noam Chomsky, *Syntactic Structures* (The Hague: Mouton, 1957).

gling to say 'the shop is closed', try 'the shop is not open', 'the man in the shop is not there', 'the man in the shop sleeps', or 'we can't buy from the shop now'. The more limited our vocabulary and structures, the harder our imagination has to work to find a possible path of communication. Gesticulations, miming, imitation (and a sense of humour!) are all indispensable tools. The more we allow our creativity a free rein, the more resources we find at our disposal.

Tips to expand your creative thinking

'Imagination is more important than knowledge' Albert Einstein
Here are a few exercises to help you expand your creative thinking:

1 Take an everyday object, no matter how insignificant, i.e. an earring, cotton wool bud, flower pot, crane, dustbin lid etc. and think of all the different uses it could be put to. Give your imagination a free rein and write down even the most absurd ideas that come to mind. Time yourself for exactly 2 minutes and see how many different ideas you can come up with. For example a dustbin lid may be used as a drum, a wheel, a tray, an umbrella etc.

2 Take two objects from within your field of vision which initially appear to be totally unrelated i.e. a pencil and a picture frame. Now think of 10 things that they have in common. Then think of 10 differences they have. Once again do not try to edit your ideas, just write down everything that comes to mind. For example a pencil and a picture frame are both hard, made of wood, breakable, etc.

2 Take any complex problem i.e. how to market a new product, how to organise a children's party, what car to buy, where to go on holiday etc. and instead of brainstorming all the things that you should – or could – do, think of all the things that you shouldn't do. Once you have made a list of all the ways how not to solve your problem, turn each idea around. This may then provide you with fresh ideas and new solutions.

A good example of the use of creative thinking is highlighted by the game 'Pictionary'.[3] If you had to draw a picture to convey the concept of 'irritation' what would you draw? An angry boss with an employee? A mother with a naughty child? A piece of grit in the eye? Someone in a slow-moving traffic jam? When your knowledge of a language is basic, the ability to view a situation from many sides will carry your communication skills a very long way.

So, with these principles in mind and with your creative resources on tap, we can move on. By revealing the multitude of similarities that exist between English and other Western European languages, you will see that the language barrier is not nearly as formidable as you may think.

---

3   Pictionary is a board game where people draw cards with various words on them. They then have to draw a picture for their partners that makes their partner think of the word on the card. They have only a couple of minutes to complete the task.

LOOK ON THE POSITIVE SIDE, WE'VE LEARNT THE MEANING OF THE WORDS 'RANSACK' AND 'SLAUGHTER' TODAY

Chapter Two

A Brief History of the English Language

Have you ever wondered why the words for 'mother' in English, German, Spanish – even Sanskrit – all start with an 'm'? Whether the expression 'the exception proves the rule' really does make sense? Where the word 'marshmallow' came from? And where the word 'striptease' went?

The archaeologist gains an insight into mankind's past through the study of ancient artefacts, sculptures and paintings. Their design and fabric give him clues about our former lifestyles and experiences, and about the many clans and cultures that have influenced and moulded our own. A cave painting of pyramids, drawn by African bushmen thousands of years ago, leads him to investigate the influences of the Egyptians. The adoption of a new metal or dye, unavailable locally, implies trading links with other tribes – as does the sudden appearance of a new weapon, symbol or word.

But archaeology is not the only science that reveals a picture of our past. Etymology – the study of the history of words – gives us a very interesting picture too.

In order to describe the changes in the world around us languages are constantly evolving, and this usually means adopting a steady stream of new expressions and words. Traditionally, languages underwent the greatest changes at times of conflict. When one culture was confronted, or colonised, by another it was often faced with a bewildering array of foreign features – clothing, foodstuffs, traditions and so on. Never having encountered such things before, their language rarely had the right words to describe them and so people slowly started to borrow the vocabulary from the languages of these foreign cultures.

For centuries, Britain was invaded and colonised by our European neighbours and today their history and languages are intrinsically linked with our own. It should therefore come as no surprise that the word 'guillotine' was originally French or that the word 'ransack' was borrowed from the Vikings.

By contrast, although colonisation today is far less frequent, the world is becoming increasingly international. People travel globally, bringing back their experiences together with a new range of vocabulary to describe them. Words such as *gorilla*, *gorgonzola*, *ginseng* and *gismo* have all arrived hand in hand with the phenomena they describe. Languages directly reflect experience, which is the reason why one Eskimo language has 42 different words for snow and some African languages have none. A Zulu tribe, whose people used the colours of the undergrowth to help navigate their way across the country, is reputed to have had 39 separate words for the colour green.

Exploring the origins of words in the English language not only reveals the influences other cultures have had on our own, but also allows us an invaluable insight into the languages they spoke and – to a large extent – still speak today.

Indo-European Languages

It is widely acknowledged that English shares its ancestry with a number of European and Asian languages. However, there is still some debate as to where our early ancestors came from and many believe that our languages date back eight or nine thousand years to a tribe of Neolithic farmers in central Asia Minor. As the population expanded, small groups broke away from the main tribe in search of new hunting grounds and food supplies, taking with them not only a common heritage but also a common language. Slowly these early Indo-Europeans migrated across Asia and Europe; some moved into Italy and Greece, others into Russia and another group made their way southwards through Afghanistan, Iran and India. Almost everywhere they went these tribes appeared to dominate the local people and impose their own culture and language. Their languages then slowly started to develop separately, absorbing words from the indigenous people they met and adapting to the differing environments in which the speakers found themselves. This process would repeat itself through the ages as the tribes dispersed into ever smaller groups and their languages adapted to reflect their individual experiences. Today we recognise these languages as the Germanic clan of German, English, Dutch, Danish, Swedish and Norwegian. Among the Romance family of languages are French, Italian, Spanish and Portuguese. Greek, Latin and Gaelic – even Hindi, Sanskrit and Persian – are also part of our extended language family.

Some of these languages (such as Italian and Spanish, or Danish and German) bear striking similarities, having broken away from each other at a later stage in history or met up again to reassert their influences. Others appear to have no similarities at all. Nevertheless, a little excavation reveals shreds of common vocabulary that leave etymologists in no doubt that all these languages go back to the same tribe of Indo-Europeans.

Take a look at the similarities between the words: 'mother', 'new' and 'three':

English	*mother*	*new*	*three*
Gaelic	*máthair*	*nua*	*tri*
French	*mère*	*nouveau*	*trois*
Spanish	*madre*	*nuevo*	*tres*
Portugese	*mãe*	*novo*	*três*
Italian	*madre*	*nuovo*	*tre*
Latin	*mater*	*novus*	*tres*
German	*Mutter*	*neu*	*drei*
Dutch	*moeder*	*nieuw*	*drie*
Danish	*mor*	*ny*	*tre*

Polish	*matka*	*nowy*	*trzy*
Greek	*meter*	*neos*	*treis*
Sanskrit	*matar*	*nava*	*trayas*
Persian	*mādar*	*nau*	*se*

The Celts and the Anglo-Saxons

The origins of the English language usually refer back to the middle of the fifth century when a number of Germanic tribes, including the Angles and the Saxons, began a long exodus to Britain. They rowed across the North Sea from what is present-day Denmark and north-west Germany to find an island populated by Celtic tribes who had inhabited the country for almost a thousand years. Although the Celts had lived under Roman rule for centuries, the Romans had left little mark on their language and the only permanent linguistic sign of their presence proved to be the place names of some of their settlements: *Chester*, for example, is derived from the Latin word for 'camp', *castra*. With the arrival of the Anglo-Saxons, Celtic communities were assimilated, destroyed or gradually pushed to the westernmost fringes of the British Isles. Here, the Celtic influence can be seen clearly in the Gaelic, Manx, Cornish and Breton languages.

The Anglo-Saxons introduced a Germanic language that was to form the basic building blocks of the English we know today. Words such as *eat, drink, speak, work, house, door, man* and *woman* were all introduced at this time and helped to form the language of Old English.

In A.D. 597 boats of Roman missionaries landed along the Kent coast and, over the next 200 years, the English language was gradually embellished with a number of Latin-based expressions. *Martyrs, demons* and *angels* all arrived in the English language at this time, as did *lentils, cucumbers* and *marshmallows*. Then, at the end of the eighth century, Europe was thrown into turmoil with the great Danish (Viking) invasions. Anglo-Saxon villages were *ransacked*, people were *slaughtered* (words of Nordic origin), and the English language bore the scars and trophies of battle with the adoption of words such as *ugly, anger, take, scream, crawl, skull*[4] and *die* and, curiously, *law* and *trust*!

The Vikings

Perhaps of little consolation to the Anglo-Saxons at that time, their language was not dissimilar to that spoken by the Vikings, as both languages were of Germanic origin. Over time common words had developed separately in both Anglo-Saxon English and Old Norse (the Germanic ancestor of modern Scandinavian languages). As the people and languages met again, certain pairs of words started to appear in the English language. *No* and *nay, shriek* and *screech, ditch* and *dike, bask* and *bathe, raise* and *rear, shirt* and *skirt* have all originated from the same source.[5]

> **Some Old English words borrowed from the Scandinavian**
>
> *Are, awkward, bank, birth, broth, brink, bull, call, clip, dirt, dregs, egg, fellow, freckle, get, give, guess, harbour, hit, ill, keel, keg, knife, leg, low, meek, muck, raise, ransack, reindeer, root, rotten, rugged, scab, scare, score, scowl, sister, sky, slaughter, sly, steak, take, thrust, trust, want, weak, window*
>
> **What pictures do these words paint of Viking culture at this time?**

After an unexpected victory for the Anglo-Saxons in 878, a treaty divided England, giving the south to the Anglo-Saxons and the north to the Vikings. The dividing line runs between London and Chester and to this day the division in dialects is quite clear. The linguistic influence can still be seen in the 1,400 place names in northern England of Scandinavian origin. Over 600 places end

---

4   Most English words with *sk* sounds have entered the English language from the Viking languages.
5   As the stems of many English and Norse words were very similar, the words were slowly amalgamated over the years to make communication easier. In the process words were simplified, endings were often lost and the English nouns adopted a generic article 'the'. This aspect of British grammar compares starkly with, for example, the three German articles for 'the': *der, die* or *das*.

in *-by*, the Danish word for farm or town (e.g. Derby, Rugby, Grimsby). Many others end in *-thorpe*, meaning village (e.g. Althorp, Linthorpe, Scunthorpe) or *-toft*, a piece of ground (e.g. Lowestoft and Nortoft). The Viking presence also influenced surnames, in particular all those ending in *-son*. To this day the majority of surnames such as Thomson, Anderson, Johnson, Davidson are still found north of this ninth century divide. In all, over 1800 words are thought to have entered the English language during this period, most of which are used today and often easily recognised in modern Germanic languages. (See chapter 5).

The Norman Conquest

In 1066 a further period of turbulence awaited the English language with the Norman Conquest. The Normans were in fact 'Men of the North', Vikings who had settled in northern France after their invasion of the territory. However, unlike the Vikings who ransacked England, their language and culture had slowly disintegrated and, by the time they arrived in England, they had become French in both manner and speech.[6]

The Normans established themselves as the ruling classes and for the next 300 years Norman French became the language of the British *aristocracy* (Frn). The Normans introduced many of the more sophisticated traditions of the French and Latin cultures to Britain, and with them came the words and expressions to describe them. The arrival of *dukes, duchesses, counts* and *countesses, courtiers, jurors* and *governors* glamorised the English language with the language of the *beau monde* (Frn). For hundreds of years, the lifestyle of the Normans tended to differ greatly from that of the *peasants*

---

6   One example of a Viking word that underwent a transformation is the Old Norse word 'skib', meaning ship, which became 'équipe' in French, meaning team. To understand this change of meaning it is important to understand the role of teams in rowing the Viking ships. Today the word 'équipe' has been extended to denote a team in general.

(Frn) who, at this stage, were primarily of Anglo-Saxon or Scandinavian origin, and the two languages coexisted. French became the language of the ruling classes, Parliament and the court, while Old English remained the language of the people. (It was not until 1362, due to growing antagonism between France and England and a subsequent rise in English patriotism, that English was used in an official opening of Parliament.) Gradually a new English emerged as the national language, having added thousands of French words to its basically Germanic structure. Around 10,000 French words entered the English language during this period, mostly to do with the mechanisms of law and administration, but many also from more general fields such as art and fashion. Over 7000 of these words are still in use in the English of today, and the majority – despite some change in spelling and pronunciation – are easily recognisable in modern French, Italian and Spanish.

Although modern English has absorbed words and expressions from both the Germanic and Romance languages, the word origins of distinct layers of vocabulary still clearly reflect the differences in British society in the Middle Ages.

The Norman French nobility ushered in *painters* and *tailors*, *scholars* and *scribes* (Frn), while the so-called Anglo-Saxon *peasants* (Frn) worked on the *land* with the *plough* and the *axe* (Gmc). They were the *blacksmiths* and the *wheelwrights*, the *hangmen* and the *gravediggers* (Gmc). These lower classes would raise *calves*, keep *cows* and hunt *swine* and *deer* (Gmc). Having *slaughtered* (Gmc) them they would then appear before their French-speaking *masters* as succulent sides of *beef* and *veal*, *bacon* and *venison* (Frn).

The Anglo-Saxon peasant would live in a *house* (Gmc), rather than a *castle* (Frn) and sit on a *stool* drawn up to a *board* (Gmc)[7] perched on supports. He would drink *ale* and eat *meat* and *bread and dripping* (Gmc). In the meantime his *master* would sit on a *chair* at a *table* and feast on *roast pork* and *mustard*, *grapes* and *biscuits* (Frn).

---

7   Think of expressions such as 'half-board', 'boarding house' and 'above-board'.

Some Middle English words borrowed from the French

Administration
Bailiff, baron, chancellor, council, court, government, liberty, mayor, minister, noble, parliament, peasant, prince, revenue, royal, squire, tax, traitor, treasurer, tyrant

Religion
Abbey, baptism, cathedral, charity, clergy, communion, confess, crucifix, friar, immortality, mercy, miracle, prayer, religion, salvation, vicar, virgin, virtue

Law
Accuse, adultery, arson, attorney, bail, blame, convict, crime, evidence, fine, gaol, heir, judge, jury, justice, pardon, plea, prison, punishment, sue, verdict, warrant

Military
Ambush, archer, army, battle, captain, combat, defend, enemy, guard, lieutenant, moat, navy, peace, retreat, sergeant, siege, soldier, spy, vanquish

Fashion
Brooch, button, cloak, collar, diamond, dress, embroidery, emerald, fashion, gown, jewel, ornament, pearl, petticoat, robe

Food and drink
Appetite, bacon, beef, biscuit, dinner, feast, grape, gravy, jelly, lettuce, mustard, veal, mutton, orange, pork, roast, salad, salmon, saucer, sausage, spice, treacle, vinegar

Learning and art
Art, beauty, geometry, grammar, image, medicine, music, painting, poet, romance, sculpture, story, surgeon

General
Adventure, bucket, ceiling, chess, chimney, conversation, curtain, cushion, flower, gay, kennel, mountain, ocean, ointment, people, please, reason, scarlet, spaniel, wardrobe

What pictures do these words paint of French culture at this time?

Now compare the similarities to modern English of these words taken from modern Danish and modern French.

Danish	French
hus (house)	*château* (castle)
stul (chair)	*chaise* (chair)
bord (table)	*table* (table)
ko (cow)	*boeuf* (cow)
swin (pig/swine)	*porc* (pig)
smed (smith)	*tailleur* (tailor)
plovmand (ploughman)	*peintre* (painter)
brød og dryppen (bread and dripping)	*biscuits* (biscuits)

As modern German is very closely linked to Danish – just as Spanish and Italian are of the same immediate family as French, learners of all these languages are often able to draw parallels from the examples above.

In understanding British history and how other cultures have affected English vocabulary we can start to guess which words we will find in each language family.

Modern influences on the English Language

In the fifteenth century the European Renaissance turned its focus on the culture and history of our Greek and Roman ancestors. Scholarship flourished, and academics and writers alike turned towards Latin as their vehicle of expression. The English language was now refined by a scattering of Latin words such as *stimulus, genius, arena, dexterity* and a number of medical and philosophical terms of Greek origin, such as *cardiograph, gynaecologist, philosophy* and *misanthropy etc.* Allowing for small changes in spelling, such words are usually identical in all Western European languages, as in these examples:

Philosophy – English	*Filosofía* – Spanish
Philosophie – French	*Filosofia* – Portuguese
Filosofia – Italian	*Philosophie* – German
Filosofi – Danish	*Filosofie* – Dutch

With the advent of the Single Market and the ever-increasing movement of people and goods in recent years, the English language continues to borrow extensively from those of her European neighbours, and vice-versa. Much to the disdain of language purists the French language now parades expressions such as *le weekend, le strip-tease, les blue-jeans* and *le chewing gum*.

Today the English language is generally regarded as one of the richest in the world. Colonisation, exploration and the exciting process of internationalisation have further studded the English language with an exotic assortment of words and phrases: *sofa* (Arabic), *kiosk* (Turkish), *veranda* (Hindi), *banana* (Guinean), *chimpanzee* (Angolan), *tea* (Mandarin), *marmalade* (Portuguese), *robot* (Czech), *amok* (Malaysian) and *assassinate* (Arabic).

Latter influences on English from other European Languages

French
tête-à-tête, savoir faire, laissez faire, joie de vivre, faux pas, rendez-vous, carte blanche, fait accompli, coup d´état, nouveau riche, hors d'oeuvre, R.S.V.P.

Spanish
cargo, siesta, sombrero, mesa, hacienda, patio, plaza, rodeo, vainilla, embargo, armadillo, bonanza

Italian
incognito, umbrella, malaria, fresco, vendetta, inferno, casino, studio, volcano, gondola, spaghetti, broccoli, macaroni, piano, opera, sonata, solo, trio

German
schnitzel, blitz, kindergarten, dachshund, poodle, lager, wanderlust, pumpernickel, hamburger

---

Meanings change with time

As words are carried through the centuries, adapted by one language, assimilated by the next, distorted by accents and misinterpretations, they often change their spelling and their original meanings. Still, there are usually enough clues left to be able to retrace the trail. One interesting word is *assassin*, which is derived from the name of the drug *hashish*. A tribe of Persians in the eleventh century were known as *the haššiši* or 'hashish eaters' for their practice of attempting to heighten their sensitivity by smoking the drug before battle. Their infamy then helped bring the word forward into the dictionaries of the twentieth century with its meaning slightly modified through time. The *proof* once meant the test (hence 'the *proof* of the pudding is in the eating' and 'the exception *proves* the rule'). *Sly* once meant wise, a *cheater* was a rent collector and the word *politician* used to refer to someone of suspicious character – a schemer or intriguer (which perhaps is not the best example of a word changing its meaning!). *Treacle* is derived from a term referring to wild animals.[8]

> **Be nice**
>
> Always a slightly dubious word, *nice* has taken on numerous guises over the past millennium. In the twelfth century *nice* was synonymous with 'stupid' or 'foolish'; over the years it has come to mean successively 'extravagant', 'slothful', 'unmanly', 'luxurious', 'modest', then 'dainty'; only in 1769 did it take on the meaning it has today as 'pleasant' and 'agreeable'.

A modern example of fashionable changes in word meanings is 'wicked' which, in slang, has come to mean 'brilliant'.

History and language tend to develop hand in hand and, when cultures share a common past, their languages almost always have some shared roots. An understanding of our own language, its origins and idiosyncrasies, can therefore be a great help when starting to learn the next – especially when it is a member of the same language family. Of course etymology (the study of the history of words) is not just an invaluable tool to help us learn foreign languages but it can also be a fun, fireside science used to reveal all sorts of interesting and quirky details about our past. It goes without saying that it also helps us to enrich our language skills in our own mother tongue.

---

[8] The world originally came from the Greek *thēriakē* – a venomous animal. *Treacle* was once the salve against venomous bites from such animals; a sticky sweet substance of mixed herbs which has slowly lost its medicinal properties but allows us the delights of treacle tarts!

SORRY, YOU HAVE TO BE IN THE MAGIC CIRCLE TO LEARN THE SECRETS OF ENGLISH GRAMMAR

Chapter Three
A Brief Tour of English Grammar

'Language is a palette of sounds, a dictionary of words made up of those sounds and a grammar of rules for combining the words meaningfully.'

Andrew Dalby, *Dictionary of Languages*, Bloomsbury 1998

We all know the saying that once you have learned one language it is easier to learn the next. Yet we rarely take into consideration the fact that we have *already* mastered the first language.

The point is that we don't *consciously* set out to learn our mother tongue. It comes upon us in a series of fits and starts and, by the time we are four or five, it becomes a natural – if somewhat clumsy – extension of our thoughts. Of course, we continue to refine language skills throughout our lives: we learn the art of charm and manipulation, we smooth-talk our way into relationships and weasel our way out of them. But only occasionally do we reflect upon exactly how it is done. How do we organise the words in a sentence? Do we use 'he' or 'him'? When do we use 'we have washed the car', and when do we merely say 'we washed it'? Having learned these details unquestioningly as a child, we quite understandably take them for granted – until we learn a foreign language.

Unfortunately, most people only first understand these structures in English when they learn a foreign language. This chapter will try to reverse the situation, providing a quick overview of the structures in the English language so that you will know what to look for in the next. (The glossary of terms and abbreviations at the back of this book will help you with the terminology in this section.)

No Frills Grammar

Very simply, in almost every sentence somebody or something does something to somebody or something else.

> i.e. *The dogs eat the chicken.*   *She sings the sonata.*
> *The twins like the doctors.*   *The baker makes them.*
> *Fernando meets Lauren.*   *They welcome her.*

In these sentences there are three main parts:

> **a subject** – the person or thing that carries out the action
> *(the dogs, the twins, Fernando, the baker, she, they)*
>
> **a verb** – the word that describes the occurrence of an action or condition
> *(eat, like, meets, sings, makes, welcome)*
>
> **an object** – the person or thing that receives the action
> *(the chicken, the doctors, Lauren, sonata, them, her)*

However, further scrutiny shows there is a fourth piece of information to be gleaned from these sentences, namely, a sense of time – or what we call **a tense**. All these sentences talk of something happening now. If they were to talk of something happening in the past or in the future, the form of the **verb** would change.

> i.e. *The dogs <u>have eaten</u> the chicken.* (past)
> *She <u>will sing</u> the sonata.* (future)
> *Fernando <u>is going to meet</u> Lauren.* (future)
> *The baker <u>made</u> them.* (past)

In summary, most basic sentences give the following pieces of information:

>a **subject noun**
>
>a **verb**
>
>an **object noun**
>
>a **tense** – reflected in the various forms of the **verb**.

As subjects and objects are invariably **nouns** (i.e. *the dogs, the chicken, the twins, Fernando, the baker, etc.*) or **pronouns** (noun substitutes such as *she, they, her* or *them*) we can conclude simply that basic sentences always contain **nouns** and **verbs**:

Nouns

The subject
If the subject is a simple **noun** – a word used to name a person, thing or concept, (i.e. *the dogs, the baker, Fernando etc.*) – it should cause few problems. Nouns in most languages are easily looked up in a dictionary and usually used as they are without causing confusion. Such nouns are context bound and can be gradually added to your vocabulary with time and need.

However, the subject could also be a **subject pronoun** – a substitute for a noun which helps to avoid constant repetition (i.e. *I, you, he, she, it, we* or *they*). These will have an equivalent in each language and, as they are used time and time again, need to be learned from the outset.

>i.e. *The dogs* have eaten the chicken and *they* have also eaten the cakes.
>*The cake* smells good and *it* tastes good, too.

The object
The object is also either a **noun** or an **object pronoun**. The nouns are, once again, easy to lift directly from the dictionary. Object pronouns

such as *her, them, me, you, him* or *us* can also be learned in time but if the memory struggles at the beginning you can always get round them by repeating the name of the person or object they represent.

    i.e. *The baker makes the <u>cakes</u>.*   –   *The baker makes <u>them</u>.*
    They welcome <u>Lauren</u>.   –   *They welcome <u>her</u>.*

In short, nouns – be they subject or object – should cause you little problem and time should not be spent learning lists of vocabulary which can only be used in very specific situations. As anyone who has played the game of Pictionary will realise, the majority of nouns are visual: think of 'chicken', 'train', 'shoe' or 'cakes'. If you don't know the word, a touch of amateur dramatics often enables them to be mimicked or mimed. Such nouns are often context-bound and, even if our acting talents fail us, the chances are that they can be pointed out directly, sketched on a piece of paper or quite simply looked up in the dictionary.

'a' or 'the'

In English, nouns are usually preceded by 'the', otherwise known as the **definite article** or 'a', known as the **indefinite article**. Other languages may have several variations of the words 'the' and 'a' such as in French *le* or *la* and *un* or *une* – the former, masculine and the latter, feminine.

Verbs

Verbs are arguably the most important words in the sentence. They are words that describe the occurrence of an action or condition (i.e. *eat, talk, sing, make, have*). Verb forms can change according to **who** is doing the action (notice the difference in English between *the dogs <u>eat</u> the chicken* and *the dog eat<u>s</u> the chicken*) and they often change according to **when** the action

> **Starting off by learning a structural equivalent to *I have lived, I live* and *I will live* in a foreign language will cover most eventualities.**

is done (*the dogs <u>have eaten</u> the chicken; the dogs <u>are eating</u> the chicken* or *the dogs <u>will eat</u> the chicken*).

Verbs are used again and again in numerous situations. The information they give about the person doing the action[9] and about the timing of the action (i.e. past, present or future tense) is usually vital to the sense of the sentence. Unlike nouns, verb forms are extremely difficult to glean from a dictionary so it is imperative that you learn them from the outset.

Verb tenses

Languages usually have several ways of saying something in the past, present or future. In English, to describe something in the past tense we can use numerous constructions: *I lived, I have lived, I was living, I have been living etc.* They all have slightly different meanings depending on the context, but if we use *I lived* in a sentence where it would be more natural to use *I have lived,* we would be understood.

At the outset it is important to learn a range of basic skills which can help us convey the majority of our ideas and experiences. In this light, it seems a far better idea to learn just *one* past, *one* present and *one* future structure than to spend the same amount of time learning the subtleties between three different past tenses and leaving yourself unable to talk about future events. The subtleties of the various other verb tenses can be learned slowly and accommodated with time.

The Frills

Once you have an appreciation of the basic make-up of simple sentences you can then adorn them with less important information. Now we can add colour and mood to our basic nouns and verbs with a range of **adjectives** and **adverbs.**

---

9   This is not so important in English as the verb usually only changes slightly in the third person – *I eat* but *he eat<u>s</u>*. In other European languages the verb tends to change a lot more depending on the person and can cause confusion if the wrong form of the verb is used.

An **adjective** adds descriptive information to the noun.

> i.e. *The <u>black</u> dogs have eaten the <u>roast</u> chicken.*
> *The <u>old</u> baker makes <u>delicious</u>, <u>hot</u> cakes.*

An **adverb** quite logically adds more information about the verb.

> i.e. *The dogs eat the chicken <u>quickly</u>.*
> *She sings the sonata <u>beautifully</u>.*

Adjectives

Adjectives change minimally in some languages depending on what they are describing, but at first you should be able to use them straight from the dictionary without too many communication problems. One characteristic you should look out for is that the adjectives in Romance languages tend to come after the noun and not before, as in English. Think of *carte blanche* and *chicken supreme*.

Adverbs

Adverbs (usually ending in –'ly' in English) tend to have a set form in most Western European languages, and can normally be lifted straight out of a dictionary.

Two Vital Conversation Techniques

1. Asking questions

One important mechanism to add to our communication skills (and one often under-employed in our own language) is the ability to ask questions.

Questions are often formed in English by a simple inversion of the sentence:[10]

> *The dogs <u>will eat</u> the chicken.* — <u>*Will*</u> *the dogs <u>eat</u> the chicken?*
> *The baker <u>has made</u> the cakes.* — <u>*Has*</u> *the baker <u>made</u> the cakes?*

You can then simply add an appropriate question word to the beginning of the sentence: *what, when, who, where, why, how* etc. The equivalents of these words are important to learn in a foreign language as they are used repeatedly.

<blockquote>
<u>When will</u> the dogs <u>eat</u> the chicken?
<u>Why has</u> the baker <u>made</u> the cakes?
</blockquote>

Simple mechanisms such as these – usually involving a simple change of word order – exist in the other European languages. As in English, raising your voice at the end of a sentence, even without changing the word order, can have the affect of changing a statement into a question.

2. Saying 'No'
The ability to say 'no' is obviously a vital addition to our language skills. When we make our sentences negative in English we tend to use the word 'not' next to the verb – as in the sentence, *the dogs have eaten the chicken – the dogs have <u>not</u> eaten the chicken*. In other European languages there is often a similar mechanism.

Skeletons in the Grammar Cupboard

Skeletons in the grammar cupboard are not so easily laid to rest. We cannot ignore memories of the **irregular verb** – the curse of all language learners!

Most verbs conform nicely to the structures previously mentioned: these, such as *I live, I lived, I have lived* and *I play, I played, I have played*, are known as **regular verbs** because they end in –'ed'

---

10 In English we also use the word 'do' in various ways. We sometimes use it to ask questions *i.e. <u>Do</u> you drink wine?* – and sometimes to transform sentences into the negative *i.e. You <u>don't</u> drink wine*. Other Western European languages don't have an equivalent of 'do'. Their question forms mainly use a change in word order, and their negatives, the simple insertion of a word equivalent to 'not'.

in the past tense. However, there are many irregular verbs, which do not follow the same patterns and unfortunately tend to be those verbs we use most.[11] Consider, for example, *I eat, I ate, I have eaten* or *I drink, I drank, I have drunk*. These are major stumbling blocks for foreigners trying to learn English and, in turn, are the areas that cause us most frustration when learning other languages. If it is any consolation the verbs that are irregular in English tend to be irregular in other Western European languages, so you may at least be able to anticipate the problem coming. Although many irregular verbs follow similar patterns, most simply have to be learned by rote, and if this means chanting them in the car or in the bath to inscribe them on your memory – so be it!

I have tried to make this whirlwind tour of the English grammar as straightforward as possible. We use these same basic structures time and time again with a number of variable details clamped on to the main frame. Parallel structures can be identified in French, Spanish, Italian, German, Dutch etc., and their fundamental similarities and differences will be highlighted in the following chapters.

---

11 The reason why the most common verbs tend to be the most irregular is because they are the ones that people spoke everyday. They are often the oldest elements of our language and of Germanic origin. In this respect their irregularities were deeply ingrained in everyday speech and could not be ironed out when grammarians tried to standardise the language centuries later.

Examples of some mistranslations made by foreigners

At a Roman Gynaecologist's:
Specialist in women and other diseases

At a Paris hotel:
Please leave your values at the front desk

In a Japanese hotel:
You are invited to take advantage of the chambermaid

In an Italian laundry:
Ladies, leave your clothes here and spend the afternoon having a good time

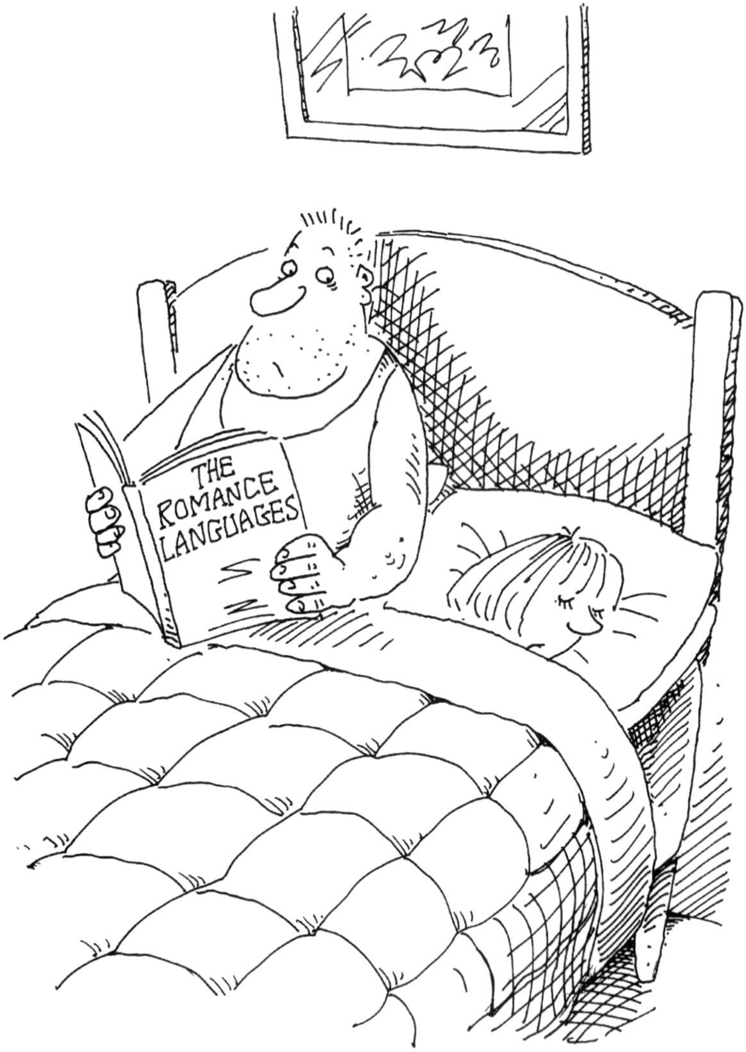
THE
ROMANCE
LANGUAGES

Chapter Four

Breaking the Barrier: The Romance Languages

Several hundred years B.C. the villagers of a small settlement on the banks of the river Tiber spoke a strange Indo-European dialect. Today their descendants sip *cappuccino* and twiddle forks of *spaghetti alla marinara* in the shadow of the Colosseum. The crumbling pillars of Rome stand testimony to one of the greatest empires the world has ever known. The cultures and languages of Europe are living proof of its previous magnitude and power.

Italian, Spanish, French, Portuguese and Romanian are all modern descendants of Latin – the language of the Roman Empire (hence the term 'Romance languages') – and they all share great similarities in vocabulary and structure. As the Empire expanded throughout the continent the Roman soldiers took with them their *chariots* and *chalices*, their *laureates* and *language*. However, the language spoken by the soldiers varied from classical Latin; they spoke a dialect known as 'vulgar' Latin. It was this language that was introduced as the new language of administration, and was slowly adopted by the indigenous peoples of the empire. By the fifth century, when the Roman Empire began to disintegrate, there were already distinct differences between the Latin spoken in one part of the continent and the Latin spoken in another. Separated from each other by great distances and daunting mountain ranges, and influenced by the speech of the local people, the languages started to evolve independently. Gradually a new generation of Romance languages was born.

The evolution of Romance languages has continued with each language borrowing heavily from various non-Romance languages.

The French language has taken much from the Germanic and Celtic languages, as have Spanish and Portuguese from the Arabic. Understandably, today it is the Italian language that most closely resembles the Latin spoken centuries before.

> 'Romance' initially referred to a mediaeval tale in Old French or Provençal describing the adventures of a hero of chivalry. This may explain the reason why the Danish word for novel is 'roman'.

Similarities between the Romance Languages

The similarities between all Romance languages are striking, even to the novice. The Spanish and the Italians, and the Spanish and the Portuguese, do not have great problems understanding each other. Having learned one Romance language you have an excellent basis for learning the next, not only as far as vocabulary is concerned, but also as far as structure and thought-processes.

For a start, the majority of English words ending in *-ion, -ary, -ible/-able* and *-ant/-ent* are very similar in all Romance languages:

English administration   necessary   possible   probable   constant   present
Italian *amministrazione*   *necessario*   *possibile*   *probabile*   *costante*   *presente*
French *administration*   *nécessaire*   *possible*   *probable*   *constant*   *présent*
Spanish *administración*   *necesario*   *posible*   *probable*   *constante*   *presente*

Understanding which words tend to be similar in English and the Romance languages gives you an immediate vocabulary of over a thousand words in French, Italian and Spanish.

Here are some more examples of words easily recognised from one Romance language to the next:

English	school	castle	escape	cost	visit
Italian	*scuola*	*castello*	*scappare*	*costa*	*visitare*
French	*école*	*château*	*échapper*	*côte*	*visiter*
Spanish	*escuela*	*castillo*	*escapar*	*costa*	*visitar*

Changes in spelling

Looking at the previous sets of words we can see that each language has put its own fingerprints on the original Latin words. Certain consonants change predictably from one language to the next – often because their sounds are very close, and easily distorted by changes in accent and spelling. Once you know which consonants are likely to differ from the English you should find it easier to detect the ultimate similarities between words.

The ph/f-changes:

English	pharmacy	telephone
Italian	*farmacia*	*telefono*
French	*pharmacie*	*téléphone*
Spanish	*farmacia*	*teléfono*

The p/b/v/f-changes:

English	lip	April	fish
Italian	*labbro*	*aprile*	*pesce*
French	*lèvre*	*avril*	*pêche*
Spanish	*labio*	*abril*	*pez*

The c/ch/k-changes:

English	change	kitchen
Italian	*cambiare*	*cucina*
French	*changer*	*cuisine*
Spanish	*cambiar*	*cocina*

The French 's'

The French language has a tendency to drop the 's' from certain words. Where it can be found in all the other languages it is often mysteriously absent from French vocabulary. Instead, an acute accent (é) may appear in its place at the beginning of the word:

école – school   *état* – state
étudier – study   *étrangler* – strangle

At other times the former presence of an 's' is indicated by the distinctive circumflex (ˆ):

côte – coast   *château* – castle
rôti – roast   *hôpital* – hospital

The Spanish 'e'
Where the French tend to omit an 's' at the beginning of the words and replace it with an *é*, the Spanish have a tendency to simply prefix the word with an *e*:

escuela – school   *estado* – state
estudiar – to study   *estrangular* – to strangle

False friends
Just to rock the apple cart here are a few 'false friends' or *faux amis*. False friends are words that often sound or look strikingly similar in two different languages, yet have different meanings. Although these words often cause problems in translation, it is often possible to see how their different meanings have evolved over time. Creatively seeking links between words and concepts is an important part of language learning.

Faux Amis		
Constipated	–	*constipado* (Sp; to have a cold)
molest	–	*molestar* (Sp; to disturb someone)
sensible	–	*sensibile* (It; sensitive)
embarrassed	–	*embarazada* (Sp; pregnant)
eventual	–	*éventuel* (Fr; possible)
prune	–	*prune* (Fr; plum)
vest	–	*veste* (Fr; jacket)

Lateral thinking

With many other words the connection to English is not always so clear. But be flexible in your thinking and explore any vocabulary that may be distantly related to the same concept. You will often find that a word of similar origin comes out of hiding. Look at the following:

> sleep: *dormire* (It), *dormir* (F), *dormir* (Sp)
> – a 'dormant' volcano
>
> horse: *cavallo* (It), *cheval* (F), *caballo* (Sp)
> – a chivalrous 'cavalier'
>
> goat: *capra* (It), *chèvre* (F), *cabra* (Sp)
> – the first sign of the zodiac is 'Capricorn'
>
> friend: *amico* (It), *ami* (F), *amigo* (Sp)
> – an 'amicable' agreement

Romantic Scaffolding

In this chapter we have addressed some of the similarities between words in various Romance languages. There are also similarities in structure, and it is at this point that the Romance languages deviate a little more from the English. Although it is obvious that we all share the common characteristics of our Indo-European forefathers, it is on the basis of structure (rather than vocabulary) that the English language is termed Germanic and not Romance.

Five differences to watch out for:
Here are five basic differences between structures found in English and those found in the Romance languages. For the sake of brevity, the examples are given in French, but the mechanisms are typical of those found in the other Romance languages.

1. Gender
The Romance languages are rather sexist, where we simply say

'the' or 'a', the Romance languages precede every noun with either a feminine or masculine article; *la* or *le* or *une* or *un*.

Where we say:
> *The* table is *green, the* cheese is *green, the* rose is *big, the* dog is *big;*

the French say:
> *La* table est *verte, le* fromage est *vert, la* rose est *grande, le* chien est *grand.*

Notice also the correspondingly small changes to the adjectives: *verte/vert* and *grande/grand*.

In English, when we talk about more than one thing we also use the generic word 'the' i.e. 'the tables' and 'the cheeses'. In French the word *les* is used in the plural; e.g. *les tables* and *les fromages*.

Although these masculine and feminine forms are used in every sentence, making an error at the beginning shouldn't cause too many misunderstandings – a *table* is always a *table*. Nevertheless, these articles crop up everywhere and their influences, although slight, are widespread.

2. Word order
Romance languages tend to put the adjective *after* the noun rather than in front of it as we do in English.

Where we say:
> *white wine, hot chocolate, a very agreeable moment* etc.;

the French say:
> *vin blanc, chocolat chaud, un moment très agréable* etc.

Nevertheless, a handful of the most common adjectives do usually remain in front of the noun – the exceptions that 'prove' the rule!

3. Double identities
The Romance languages have two different forms of address; where we simply use the word 'you', they have a formal, polite

version, which in French is *vous,* and an informal version, *tu.* Deciding which one to use can still cause problems, even for native speakers, but it is generally advisable to address anyone older or senior with *vous* and wait and see if the style of address changes to *tu* as the relationship develops. Other forms are also used when addressing a group of two people or more.

4. The personal touch
The Romance languages tend to change the verb-ending depending on the person doing the action, whereas English only usually changes in the third person – in the 'he', 'she' or 'it' form.

Where we say:	The French say:
I prepar*e*	Je prépar*e*
You prepar*e*	Tu prépar*es/* Vous prépar*ez*
He/she/it prepar*es*	Il/elle prépar*e*
We prepar*e*	Nous prépar*ons*
They prepar*e*	Ils prépar*ent*

These sensitive changes appear in all the Romance languages, and in all tenses, and although patterns repeat themselves again and again, this is one of the most important features to learn of any language. In Spanish and Italian, as the verbs change clearly depending on who they are referring to, and the pronunciation of the words makes these changes very clear, there is little need for the pronouns ('he', 'she', 'we' etc.). These are often omitted in Spanish and Italian.

5. Word endings
The Romance languages tend to change verb endings, depending on who is being referred to and also when the action is being done. In English we tend to use a separate word (**auxiliary verb**) in front of the main verb.

Where we say:
 I will eat, I will dance and *I was eating, I was dancing;*

the French say:
Je mange__rai__, Je dance__rai__ and *Je mange__ais__, Je danc__ais__*.

Although I have taken examples from the French language, they are typical examples of corresponding structures in Italian and Spanish. Once you are made aware of them you will find them time and time again. It will also be easier for you to breakdown and analyse words when you realise that many word endings have grammatical significance, but do not form part of the word's etymological root.

Other minor quirks of the Romance languages
1. Where we tend to add an 's' to denote possession, such as 'the dog's dinner', 'Caroline's party' etc., the Romance languages often use a structure equivalent to 'the dinner of the dog', 'the party of Caroline'. Most people have seen the term *vin de table* on the labels of cheap French table wines.

2. French has a strange way of counting numbers from seventy to one hundred. Seventy is *soixante-dix*, (lit. sixty and ten), eighty is *quatre-vingt* (literally four times twenty) and ninety is *quatre-vingt-dix* (literally four times twenty plus ten). However, in the past, English has also had strange ways of counting. How much was four score and ten?

Romance languages
Proverbs and expressions

Chat échaudé craint l'eau froide. (F)
  Once bitten twice shy.
  (Lit. A scolded cat fears cold water)

Chapeau! (F) Bravo, well done! (Lit. Hat!)

Ho altre gatte da pelare. (It)
  I have other fish to fry.
  (Lit. I have other cats to skin)

Avere un chiodo in testa. (It)
  To have a bee in one's bonnet.
  (Lit. To have a nail in the head)

Cuando las ranas críen pelos. (Sp)
  When pigs learn to fly!
  (Lit. When frogs grow hairs!)

Comer como una vaca. (Sp)
  To eat like a horse
  (Lit. To eat like a cow)

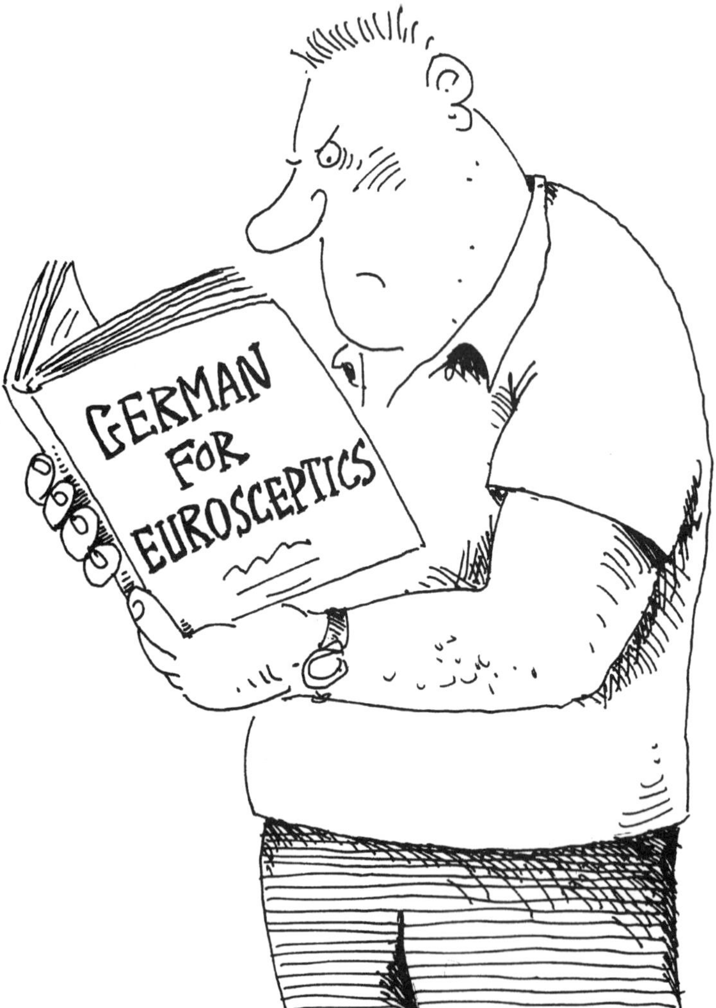
GERMAN
FOR
EUROSCEPTICS

CHAPTER FIVE
Breaking the Barrier: The Germanic Languages

It is generally believed that by the first century B.C. Germanic tribes could be found on both sides of the North and Baltic seas. At this time it appears that they all spoke a fairly uniform language, which then started to evolve into distinct regional dialects and eventually different languages. Over the next 500 years the tribes that had settled in Western Europe – east of the Rhine and north of the upper Danube – were in constant battle against the Roman Empire, eroding its frontiers and sapping its strength. The language of these *barbarians*[12] has evolved into the modern German now spoken in Germany, Austria and Switzerland. Dutch, the language of the Netherlands, has also been formed from a west German dialect. The tribes that settled to the east of the Oder spoke a language known as East German but political upheaval in the past century has brought about its extinction. Gothic provides the oldest written evidence of its existence. The Germanic tribes that moved north of the Baltic developed a language known as Old Norse – the language of the old Viking sagas – and the ancestor of Danish, Norwegian, Swedish and Icelandic.

The British Isles had been populated by the Celts up until the fifth century A.D. when the Angles, Jutes and Saxons invaded the country from the east. Scattering the Celts to the northern and western extremities of the country, their German dialects came to

---

12 The word 'Barbarian' was a term used by the Romans to describe the tribes of Germanic peoples. It comes from the Greek word meaning 'foreign' or 'uncivilised'.

form the building blocks of the English language. Together with German and Dutch, English is now classified as a West Germanic language – more in terms of its grammar than vocabulary, from which it has borrowed heavily from Old French.

Similarities between the Germanic Languages

Even to the novice, similarities between the Germanic languages are easily recognisable, and learning one language will provide a useful platform for learning the next – not only in terms of vocabulary but also in structure and thinking processes.

Here are some examples of words easily recognised from one Germanic language to the next.

English	house	hand	warm	blind	illustration	explosion
German	*Haus*	*Hand*	*warm*	*blind*	*Illustration*	*Explosion*
Dutch	*huis*	*hand*	*warm*	*blind*	*illustratie*	*explosie*
Danish	*hus*	*hånd*	*varme*	*blind*	*illustration*	*eksplosion*

You will find that most English words ending in *-ion* are similar in all Western European languages.

Changes in spelling

As you will notice, certain consonants change predictably from one language to the next – often because their sounds are very close, and easily distorted by changes in accent and spelling. Once you know which consonants are likely to differ from the English, it should be easier to detect the ultimate similarities between words. Here are some examples:

The ph/f-changes:

English	photograph	telephone
German	*Fotografie*	*Telefon*
Dutch	*fotografie*	*telefoon*
Danish	*fotografi*	*telefon*

The p/b/v/f-changes:

English	lip	live	grave	father
German	*Lippe*	*leben*	*Grab*	*Vater*
Dutch	*lip*	*leven*	*graf*	*vader*
Danish	*læbe*	*leve*	*grav*	*fader*

The t/th/d-changes:

English	bread	god	think
German	*Brot*	*Gott*	*denken*
Dutch	*brood*	*god*	*denken*
Danish	*brød*	*gud*	*tænke*

The ch/sk/k-changes:

English	milk	book	cook
German	*Milch*	*Buch*	*Koch*
Dutch	*melk*	*boek*	*kok*
Danish	*mælk*	*bog*	*kok*

Compound words

One common characteristic of Germanic languages is to make new words by compounding existing words rather than borrowing from other languages as English often does. Where English has invented the word 'television' from the Greek and Latin words meaning 'far' and 'to see', German has, for example, called it a *Fernseher* (a purely German compound meaning 'far-seer'). Here are some other examples of compound words:

glove: *Handschuh* (G), *handschoen* (Du), *handske* (Da)
(lit. a 'hand-shoe')
dictionary: *Wörterbuch* (G), *woordenboek* (Du), *ordbog* (Da)
(lit. a 'word-book')
sunrise: *Sonnenaufgang* (G), *zonsopgang* (Du), *solopgang* (Da)
(lit. a 'sun-up-way')

Another striking characteristic of Germanic languages is to make a chain of nouns and adjectives into a single word. Initially these long words may appear inscrutable, but they are often easily broken down into commonly recognised parts.

>*Orangensaftkonzentrat* (G) – concentrated orange juice
>*Volkorenbrood* (Du) – wholemeal bread
>*Naturreservat* (Da) – nature reserve
>*Technischerüberwachungsverein* (G) – The Technical Insurance Association (Literally 'the technical over-watching association') or T. Ü. V. or M. O. T. (English equivalent)

Germanic Scaffolding

There are many similarities in structure between the Germanic languages but there are also some differences. German grammar differs most strikingly from English in several areas, whereas Dutch and Danish at times take after the German structures and at others follow those very similar to our own. As German is the second most widely spoken Germanic language after English, this section will highlight the main differences between English and German, making references to the other languages when necessary.

Five basic differences to watch out for:
Here are five basic differences between English and German grammar:

1. Gender
German, like French, is rather sexist; where we simply say 'the' or 'a', the German precedes every noun with either a feminine, masculine or neuter article: *die, der* or *das* or *eine* and *ein*.[13]
   Where we say:
      the man is *big*, *the* cat is *big*, *the* car is *big*;

---

13   Dutch and Danish only have two different forms of 'the' in the singular form.

the Germans say:
der Mann ist groß, die Katze ist große or *das Auto ist groß.*

When we talk about more than one thing we also use the generic word 'the', as in 'the men', 'the cats', 'the cars'. In German the word *die* is used in the plural, e.g. *die Männer, die Katzen* and *die Autos.*

Although these forms of 'the' are used in every sentence, making an error at the beginning shouldn't cause too many misunderstandings – a *Katze* is always a *Katze*. Nevertheless, try to learn each word and its article as a set pair.

2. Word positions

If a German noun is the subject of a sentence, the form of 'the' used may be different from when it is the object of the sentence. In English the word 'the' remains unaffected wherever it is in the sentence; we can say 'the pen is on the book' or 'the book is on the pen', and there are no changes apart from the position of the words.

In German the two sentences would read as follows.

<u>Der Stift</u> *ist auf dem Buch.*   –   The pen is on the book.
Das Buch ist auf <u>dem</u> Stift.   –   The book is on the pen.

Note the change from *der Stift* to *dem Stift*, because of its change of role in the sentence.

These changes occur in German for all three singular versions of the word 'the' as well as the one plural form. The German language recognises four different functions, or **cases**, of 'the' in the sentence, which means that there are many variants of the word 'the' (although luckily some forms do look the same). Happily, in Dutch and Danish, although there are two singular versions of 'the', and one plural form, they do not change according to their role in the sentence. Adjectives may also change in conjunction with 'the', so, depending on its position in the sentence, *groß* may be spelt *große* or *großes* or *großen*. Naturally, these cases are the bane of all German language learners and even native speakers make mistakes. Although they are relatively important, it must be stressed that making a mistake in using *die, der* or *das, groß* or *große*[14] does not usually lead to grave misunderstandings. This complex feature of German grammar will become increasingly familiar as you study the language.

3. Double identities
The Germanic languages have two different forms of address where we simply use the word 'you', they have a formal, polite version, which in German is *Sie*, and an informal version *du*. Deciding which one to use can still cause problems even for native speakers, but it is generally advisable to address anyone older or senior to yourself with *Sie* and wait to see if the style of address changes to *du* as the relationship develops.

Danish and Dutch societies are traditionally known for their egalitarianism, and they tend to use the informal style of 'you' a little more often than the Germans.

Other forms of address are also used when addressing a group of two people or more.

4. The personal touch
Germanic languages tend to change the verb with the person doing the action, whereas English only usually changes in the third person – in the 'he', 'she' or 'it' form.

Where we say:	**The Germans say:**
I have	*Ich habe*[15]
you have	*du hast/Sie haben*
He/she/it has	*er/sie/es hat*
We have	*wir haben*
They have	*sie haben*

---

14   In modern German the *-ß* is sometimes written as *-ss*.
15   Notice the v/b shift from 'have' to 'habe'.

As the verb changes according to the person, making a mistake in the verb form may lead to some confusion as to whom you are talking about. Consequently, one of the first things to do in any language is to learn the various forms of the verb. Luckily these patterns repeat themselves and most verbs take exactly the same endings time and time again.

As far as the different verb tenses are concerned in the past, present and future, the pattern of Germanic verbs is formed very much like those in English.

'I will give'   –   *Ich werde geben*[16]
'I would give'   –   *Ich würde geben*
'I gave'   –   *Ich gab*
'I have given'   –   *Ich habe gegeben*

Note the use of the prefix *ge-* in the **past participle.**

5. Word order

One of the most striking features of German and Dutch grammar is that the word order often differs dramatically from that of English, whereas the word order in Scandinavian languages is more similar. In German and Dutch there is a tendency to place the verbs at the very end of the sentence rather than in the middle as we do in English.

I have given the chocolates.
Ich habe die Schokolade gegeben.

Here is the man who has given the chocolates.
Hier ist der man der die Schokolade gegeben hat.

It has been said that this difference in word order, namely placing the verb at the very end of the sentence, makes Germans attentive listeners!

---

16 Notice again the v/b shift from 'give' to *geben*.

Other minor quirks of the Germanic languages
1. As you will have noticed, all German nouns begin with a capital letter. This is not so in Dutch and Danish.

2. When forming the plurals of words, Germanic languages do not tend to put an *'s'* on the end of the word but instead add a series of endings such as *–e, -en* etc. In addition to this the vowels in the middle of the word often change in the plural form. Although in English we tend to use the French plural form *'s'*, remnants of the Germanic plural can still be seen in English words such as *child – children, brother – brethren, woman – women.*

Another point of confusion is that when Germans say *halb-neun* (literally translated as half-nine), they actually mean half an hour *to* nine, or, as we would say in English, 'half eight'. This has undoubtedly caused many missed appointments between the British and the Germans, not to mention the Dutch and Danes who also use similar expressions.

Germanic languages
Proverbs and expressions

Wo drückt der Schuh? (G)
    What's bothering you?
    (Lit. Where does the shoe press?)

Was Hänschen nicht lernt, lernt Hans nimmermehr. (G)
    You can't teach an old dog new tricks.
    (Lit. What young Hans doesn't learn, old Hans never will)

Etwas liegt mir schwer im Magen. (G)
    It weighs heavily on my mind.
    (Lit. It lies heavily in my stomach)

Ikke sælge skindet før bjørnen er skudt. (Da)
    Don't count your chickens before they hatch.
    (Lit. Don't sell the bear skin before you shoot the bear)

Den enes død , den andens brød. (Da)
    One man's loss is another man's gain.
    (Lit. One man's death is another man's bread)

De appel valt niet ver van de boom. (Du)
    Like father like son.
    (Lit. The apple never falls far from the tree)

Het regent pijpestelen. (Du)
    It's raining cats and dogs.
    (Lit. It's raining pipestems)

estudiar
Stul
mãe
novo
Waffle
école
cocina
muck
trzy
wienerbrød
mère
huis
pez
cappuccini
caballo
ORDBOG
filosofi

Chapter Six
Action Plan

This final section of the book prepares you for action. Here you will find a plethora of study tips and focus points to start you on the road to learning a foreign language. First, however, make sure that you are confident of the reasons why you want to learn the language you have chosen. Do you simply want to be able to communicate with local people while you are travelling, to talk about the food and weather, and ask directions to the nearest post office? Do you need the language for specific business reasons, such as negotiating and making presentations - or just as a social skill to help you build rapport with business colleagues over dinner? Do you want to be able to have in-depth, complex conversations with people or to follow a profession as a linguist? Do you want the language to help you read literature in its original form? Whatever your reasons for learning a foreign language they should be clear to you from the start. With these in mind you are then able to determine just what and how much you need to learn and – just as importantly – what you *don't*.

It is also essential to have an appreciation of *how* you learn best. Do you like to focus on rules, building up your skills systematically, exercise after exercise? Do you learn best by listening and repeating what you have heard or by interacting with people (real or imaginary) and carrying out small role-plays and conversations? Most people learn using a combination of these techniques although we all seem to have preferences. On the whole, the more senses stimulated in the process, the easier it is for the brain to identify with the words, and then catalogue and recall them at a later stage.

Choosing a Language Course

There are many different types of courses to choose from. Those needing their languages for business purposes may find that their company will pay for in-house language training, but those seeking to learn languages for purely personal reasons have a variety of options to choose from. Here we take a look at the advantages and disadvantages of various courses of study.

Travelling abroad to study

If you have the time, money and dedication, a visit to the country where your language is spoken can provide an invaluable injection of enthusiasm. Not only will you hear the language spoken around you but you will also come to feel it and experience it in context. For the more widely-spoken European languages there is an endless range of language courses on offer, which can last from one week up to a year if you so wish. You may prefer to live independently or lodge with a host family during the course, and packages can be tailor-made to suit most tastes and needs. Recently, a number of more original language courses have started to sprout up where you can combine language learning with other interests such as walking, dancing or cooking and these can offer very conducive learning environments.

The advantages of studying abroad (for those with the resources to do so) are obvious. Nevertheless, there is a tendency for fellow language students to socialise together outside lessons, finding themselves in a foreign clique and insulating themselves from the surrounding culture. This can be remedied by an independent spirit, taking the decision to break away from the group and explore the local area on your own, asking for directions and information from tourist offices, shop keepers and friendly passers-by, and thereby putting your new-found skills into practice.

Adult education courses in your local town

Due to time and resources most people start by studying a foreign language for a few hours a week – either daytime or evening – and subscribe to an adult education course run at a local college or university. The advantage of such courses is that they can be easily integrated into your weekly routine, and the presence of a native teacher once again adds an important touch of authenticity, allowing students the opportunity to speak, and providing a semi-disciplined learning structure. This can also be a great place to meet like-minded people who share a common enthusiasm for the subject, which in itself can be highly motivational. Naturally, one of the drawbacks of such a course is that it is potluck whether you find an interesting group of students and, more importantly, an inspiring teacher. If you are thinking of starting such a course ask around for recommendations before you subscribe; there may be several courses in your local vicinity to choose from.

Self-study course
Teaching oneself from a language course book requires a lot of self-discipline but if you have this, then you will find yourself master of studies and can focus your energy whenever and wherever you really feel the need. Often self-study is best done in conjunction with one of the other methods described, but many people simply don't have the time to commit two evenings a week to a language course. Apart from high levels of self-discipline and motivation, studying on one's own demands that your objectives are crystal clear.

Find as many occasions as you can to go out and live the language: travel abroad if possible; eat at a restaurant where you know the staff speak the language; watch foreign TV channels and original version films; buy foreign music and try following the lyrics; or just try out monologues with yourself seeing how many sentences you can string together in an imaginary conversation. Check whether there is an institute nearby, such as the Institute Français or the Instituto Cervantes, which host theme evenings and allow you the opportunity to mix with other people of similar interests.

Finding the right self-study course is not always so easy but usually the staff in a large and reputable bookshop can give sound advice. Take time to look through the books on offer: Does the layout look easy to follow? Is there a clear and logical index and contents page? Try picking a section on, for example, 'adjectives' or 'prepositions' and compare the approach of several different authors. Choose the book that makes the most sense to you. Most textbooks have a series of exercises and answers, which enable you to monitor your progress, and offer invaluable help when studying alone. A table of irregular verbs is crucial; make sure that there is one in either your textbook or dictionary. You may even want to buy a pocket book dedicated to the verbs alone. There is also a wide variety of courses available on video and CD-ROM, which are good value for money, and being very visual and interactive are a highly recommended learning aid. It is a good idea to go to a store with a specialist language department and ask an assistant for advice.

Self-study tips

Allocate set periods of time to study. 'Later' won't do, from 8.00pm to 9.00pm is far better. Write it into your diary.

It is better to do a little at regular intervals than to do a lot spasmodically.

When you finish, close the book and brainstorm eight or more things you have just learned about the language.

When you start the next session, take a minute to glance through the pages you last studied and the notes you made. Close the book and then, once again, try to brainstorm everything you can remember.

Choosing a dictionary

When choosing a dictionary try to find one that puts the words in context. Simple word-for-word translations are not always enough and, at times, not even possible. Find a dictionary that uses the foreign word in a sample sentence, allowing you to see how it fits into the sentence structure, but also helping you to better understand the context in which it applies.

One common mistake when using a foreign-language dictionary is that people frequently pick the first word given in the translation without reading the list of explanations to the end. The danger of this is that where in English we can use the same word in very different contexts, this change in contexts in another language may dictate a change of word altogether. Once in a hardware shop in Denmark I asked for some nails (having looked the word up in my dictionary). They looked at me agog and, later, friends explained to me why. I had asked for the type of nails that go on fingers; those that go into walls are translated by a totally different word altogether. Always read through the translation of a word from start to finish to be sure to find the right explanation.

Taking your language abroad

Props
When you first travel abroad and are eager to put your language into practice, it is important to have a few props with you. A pocket notebook will always come in handy to jot down new vocabulary, directions, names and telephone numbers or even draw pictures when your acting talents fail you. It is an equally good idea to have a pocket dictionary with you for moments when you feel less artistically inclined – but try not to shackle yourself too much to it; first try to communicate using the words and phrases you have already learned and take your creative thinking for a work-out.

Learn a few of the very basic conversational phrases used in everyday interactions. Whether you have decided to study the local language or not, learning four or five simple phrases can considerably help the way you are received, and make the rest of your communication easier. When meeting new people for the first time, conversations often follow similar lines, and patterns of conversation crop up again and again. People will invariably launch conversations by making a comment about a common experience;

for example, the weather, the food, the wine or the view. If the conversation progresses, the topics of conversation may turn to homes, jobs and families. Learning a few words and expressions on these topics can be a good start, constructing them into simple sentences using the most popular verbs. There is no use learning the words for politicians, pearls and plugs when in reality you only ever talk about your family and your dog!

Getting personal
Finally one fun tip is to learn a short phrase or idiom that can be repeated in many different contexts and may just win you a smile. (When my father went to Brazil his one party piece in Portuguese was the phrase 'my children always cause me problems', which earned him the sympathy of his colleagues – if not his children!). General phrases such as, *c'est la vie* (that's life) in French or *ohne Fleiß kein Preiß* (no pain, no gain) in German or *buen provecho* (bon apetit) in Spanish may help take your interactions to a slightly more personal level. Find a simple phrase that appeals to you and look up its equivalent in a good bilingual dictionary. Then try it out.

Language-learning tips

Use what you know as a foundation for what you don't know.

Seek the bigger picture before going into detail.

Start with the most important structures and leave the least important till last.

- **Don't learn lists of nouns**
  Nouns are usually easy to retrieve from a dictionary or deduced through context.

- **Focus on learning the verbs**
  Verbs are the most important and complex part of a sentence.

- **Learn how to use verbs in one past, one present and one future tense**
  Learn the subtleties of the remaining verb tenses as you progress.

- **Learn how to change the word order and form simple questions**
  The ability to ask questions is a crucial communication skill.

- **Make sure you know how to form negative sentences**
  This is usually the simple insertion of a word equivalent to 'not'.

Twenty of some of the most important verbs to learn in a foreign language:

to be	*to have*	*to want*	*must/to need*
can (to be able to)	*to know*	*to like*	*to go*
to see	*to eat*	*to drink*	*to work*
to sleep	*to take*	*to buy*	*to think*
to speak	*to make/do*	*to pay*	*to understand*

With just these 20 verbs you can construct hundreds of useful sentences.

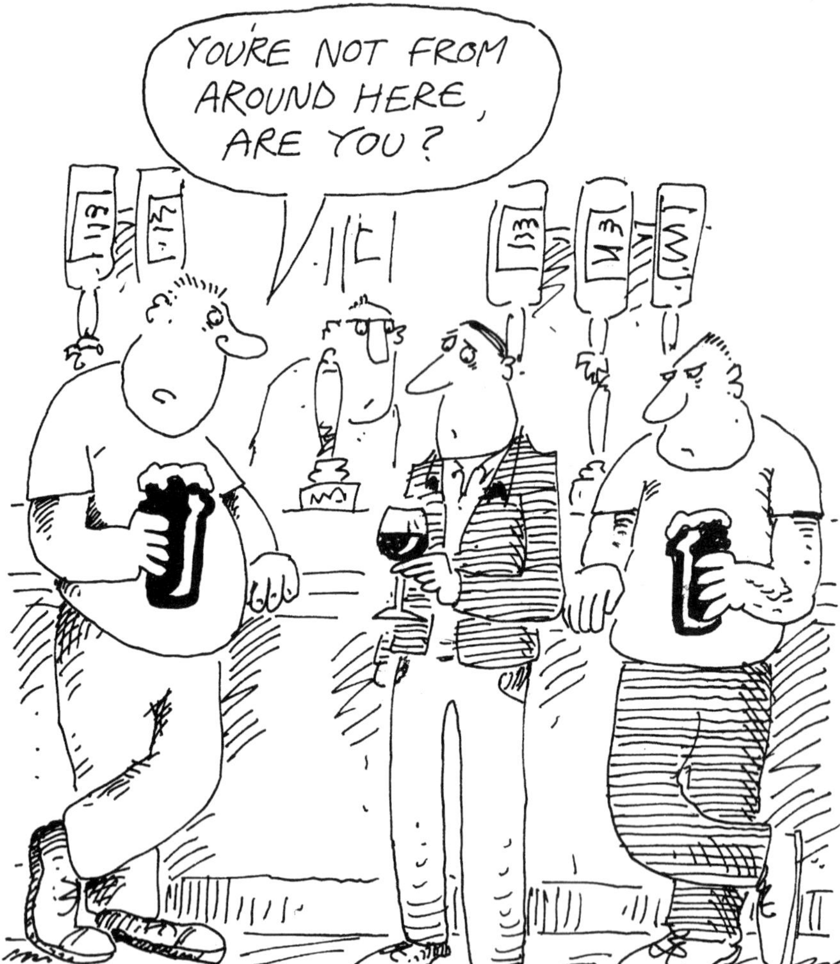
YOU'RE NOT FROM AROUND HERE, ARE YOU?

Chapter Seven

Being Culturally Aware

Words are not the only tools of communication and failing to be aware of the differences between cultures, their traditions and values, can sometimes cause far greater misunderstanding than any linguistic shortcomings. Living in France and Italy I adapted effortlessly to the tradition of greeting each other with kisses on the cheek. In some places it was two, in some three and, in others, people were insulted if you didn't give them four! I don't think I ever quite worked out which region gave which number of kisses but the important thing was to take my cue from other people and be ever ready to exchange a kiss or two. Heaven knows what the Danes thought of me when I moved to Copenhagen several years later. Here, a common greeting between friends and colleagues is the hug. Jowl to jowl in firm Viking clamps, it is never easy to see exactly what goes on and (much to my embarrassment now) I never even stopped to think. I must have kissed more Danish men during my years in Copenhagen than most Danish women do in their entire lives!

Although, in this case, my lack of understanding of social customs left me unscathed, it is easy to see how cultural insensitivity can lead to embarrassment, even offence. What irritates me is not so much the fact that I didn't know this custom but that I wasn't receptive enough to pick it up. After years of kissing the Danes I still failed to notice that none of them were kissing me!

There are many areas where potential misunderstandings

can arise. Here are some of the major arenas for cultural differences; forewarned is hopefully forearmed.

Areas of potential cultural misunderstanding

Greetings
How do people greet each other? How much, and what type of physical contact is involved? How much personal space do they need? How does this differ according to the relationships between people?

Dress
What is the usual dress code for work, dinners *en famille* or at a restaurant? How do people dress at religious festivals or on holy days? Is revealing certain parts of the body seen as disrespectful? For example, you can't go into some churches in Italy with bare shoulders yet in France you can go topless on the beaches.

Food and drink
How are people seated around a table? Who is served first? Who starts? Are there any ritualistic salutations or ceremonies connected to eating or drinking? Did you know that in Sweden people don't usually start their wine at a formal meal until their host has raised a toast and looked them solemnly in the eye for three seconds?

Money
Who pays the bill or do you split it? Can you barter? Should you pay a tip? How is the subject of money addressed? Is it talked about openly or considered an 'unsavoury' subject? Many years ago I remember paying for a day's history tour of Copenhagen. Before we left, the lecturer gave an introductory talk on the day; on the places of architectural wonder we would visit, the palaces and cathedrals, and a café where we could buy a cheap cup of coffee! At the other extreme, when paying a large restaurant bill at my

local restaurant in Spain, I received wounded stares from Teresa, the owner, when I even ventured a glance at the arithmetic.

Relationships between males and females
Do men address women differently than they address other men? Is there a set protocol for the way men should treat women in public? Or the way women should treat men? In Northern Europe opening a door for a woman can sometimes be a risky affair, and some women are likely to interpret it as an act of chauvinism. In Southern Europe, not doing so is more likely to be interpreted as bad manners.

Present giving
When are you expected to give a gift? What types of gifts are considered appropriate? In Mediterranean countries people more often tend to bring flowers and chocolates for the host of a dinner party than a bottle of wine.

Business relationships
Do you treat your superiors differently from your colleagues and subordinates? Do the different levels of the corporate hierarchy mix socially? How and where is business conducted? Who makes the decisions?

I remember an incident where an Englishman visited a German company in the hope of winning a contract. He was finally given it, and invited all the staff out for a celebratory drink. The following Monday he learned that the contract had been cancelled and only months later discovered the reason why. The directors of the German company had seen him fraternise with the junior employees and had come to mistrust him.

Although, in Western Europe, the differences between cultures are not as radical as they are between different continents, they still exist. It is easy to be lulled into a false sense of security by the ubiquitous Gucci shoes or mobile telephones, yet behind the modern veneer of Western cultures lie thousands of years of history. Religion, wars, political upheaval, immigration and geography all leave lasting fingerprints on cultures, and on people's values and perceptions. What may seem a superficial ritual to the outsider, to the insider may be an important symbol of respect.

One of the greatest skills we can learn when we travel is to be receptive; to **watch, observe** and **listen**. A few hours spent in a café in the centre of town observing the people who pass by may be as useful to your overall communication skills as tackling the next irregular verb!

Bon Voyage

I sincerely hope that you have found this book useful and now feel more confident about learning a foreign language. Personally, languages have given me an immense amount of joy; from evenings round campfires with foresters in northern Sweden, to tortellini-making sessions with a friend's grandmother in Bologna and philosophical debates with a garlic farmer while awaiting a train to Madrid. Languages have added a further dimension to my travels. I no longer measure them in distance but in depth.

We must never lose sight of the primary reasons for learning a foreign language: to provide a bridge between cultures, to open up conversations and to allow an exchange of observations, experience and human warmth. So don't let an unnecessary obsession for perfection get in the way.

Learn the basics. Learn how to ask simple questions and give simple answers, memorise a cluster of the most important verbs and have a go. I wish you all the best along the way.

Glossary

This is a short glossary of the grammatical terms used in the book:

Adjective: A word used to describe a noun or pronoun (e.g. *happy, green, sweet*).

Adverb: A word used to describe a verb or adjective (e.g. *slowly, happily, greedily*).

Article: A word before the noun (e.g. *a, the*) 'a' is known as the indefinite article, and 'the' as the definite article.

Auxiliary verb: A verb used with main verbs to show tense, mood etc.

Case: A change in the form of the noun and its article to show its relationship with another word and its role in the sentence.

Irregular verb: A verb that does not change in the usual way. A regular verb adds '-ed' in the past tense.

Noun: A word used to name a person, thing or concept *(Peter, the car, a tap)*.

Object: The direct recipient of the action described by the verb.

Past participle: A form of the verb used in certain past tenses.

Preposition: A word before a pronoun or noun to relate it to other words in the sentence (e.g. *on, off, in, out*).

Pronoun: A word substituting a noun and referring to one or more persons or objects (e.g. *she, her, he, him, they, them*).

Subject: A noun or pronoun that carries out the action described by the verb.

Tense: A category of verb which expresses a sense of time (e.g. *we will eat, we have eaten, we would eat*).

Verb: A word that expresses the performance or occurrence of an action – or occurrence of a condition (e.g. *to speak, to eat, to be, to have, to travel*).